What Color is the Sun

Kenneth Jernigan
Editor

A KERNEL BOOK
published by
NATIONAL FEDERATION OF THE BLIND

Copyright © 1991 by National Federation
of the Blind

ISBN 0-9624122-2-8

All Rights Reserved.

Printed in the United States of America

Table of Contents

Kenneth Jernigan, Executive Director
National Federation of the Blind

EDITOR'S INTRODUCTION

by Kenneth Jernigan

For at least twenty years I have been appearing on radio and television and in the newspapers as the spokesman of the National Federation of the Blind, and lately something has been happening with increased frequency which I probably should have anticipated but didn't. Total strangers keep stopping me on the street or in the supermarket or airport to ask me about blindness. Well, not exactly about blindness as such, but about what it is like to be blind—about the every day experiences and the ordinary happenings in the lives of blind people. I do the best I can to tell them, but usually neither they nor I have the time for me really to do it right. This book is an attempt to remedy that situation. Even so, I still don't know that I have done it right, but at least it is better than a hurried attempt in a supermarket.

The persons who appear in the pages of the book are people that I know—friends, former students, colleagues in the National Federation of the Blind. Mostly they tell their own stories—stories of ordinary men and women who think about last night's dinner, today's taxes, and tomorrow's hopes and dreams. These are people I think you would like to know, so I am introducing them to you. And I am also telling you a little about myself. When you have finished reading these personal accounts and reminiscences I hope you will have a better picture of what it is like to be blind and how blind people feel. Mostly we feel just about the same way you do.

Kenneth Jernigan
Baltimore, Maryland
1991

GROWING UP BLIND IN TENNESSEE DURING THE DEPRESSION

by Kenneth Jernigan

I grew up on a farm in middle Tennessee during the depression—first the farm depression and then the one that everybody talks about. Life was not the way it is today. My father (though intelligent) had less than two weeks of formal schooling, and my mother (at least equally intelligent) did not finish the eighth grade. There were no books in our home except the family Bible, and we didn't get a newspaper or magazine.

We had no radio; no telephone; and until I was six, no automobile. It was the early thirties, and money was scarce. Hogs (when we had any) brought two cents a pound; and anything else we had to sell brought an equally low price.

I had an isolated existence. Except for the extremely elderly, I was the only blind person for miles around. My experiences in no way were like those of the sighted children I knew. Mostly until I was six, I had nothing to do and nobody to play with. Sometimes on Sundays my family and I would go to the home of one or the other of my grandparents for dinner and the day. I remember those times vividly.

The men (remember that this was rural Tennessee in the early thirties) would sit under a shade tree in the front yard and talk about the crops, the weather, and the price of hogs. The women would be in the kitchen preparing Sunday dinner and talking about children, what the neighbors were doing, and their gardens.

The boys and girls (usually a bevy of cousins were there on such occasions) would be in the barnyard playing hide and seek, tag, or some other game. I belonged to none of these groups. I circulated back and forth on the edges and hoped the day would end.

One thing more: Nobody had indoor toilets, so if I knew we were going somewhere for Sunday dinner, I would begin the day before to reduce my intake of liquids. It is embarrassing for a child of five to have to interrupt the men under the shade tree to ask if someone will take him down behind the barn to answer the call of nature.

Here I am in 1933 with my older brother, Lloyd, and my dog, Wag.

I am sure that each person who attended those gatherings came away with different memories, memories that lingered through the years—playing with other children, talking with the men under the trees, or exchanging confidences in the kitchen.

Certainly I came away with memories. They revolve around a full bladder and a day of boredom. This is not to say that I felt abused or mistreated. Instead, I recognized (even at that early age) that the world was as it was; that nobody was trying to do me in; and that if I wanted to have a full life, I had better learn to plan and think ahead.

My parents loved me, but they didn't know how to deal with a blind child. They knew that they wanted the best for me, and I knew that I wanted out of that limited environment.

Every time I could, I got somebody to read to me. Read what? Anything—anything I could get. I would nag and pester anybody I could find to read me anything that was available—the Bible, an agriculture yearbook, a part of a newspaper, or the Sears Roebuck catalog. It didn't matter. Reading was magic. It opened up new worlds.

I remember the joy—a joy which amounted to reverence and awe—which I felt during those times I was allowed to visit an aunt who had books in her home. It was from her daughter (my cousin) that I first heard the fairy stories from The Book of Knowledge—a treasure which many of today's children have unfortunately missed.

My cousin loved to read and was long suffering and kind, but I know that I tried her patience with my insatiable appetite. It was not possible for me to get enough, and I always dreaded going home, finding every excuse I could to stay as long as my parents would let me.

I loved my aunt; I was fascinated by the radio she had; and I delighted in her superb cooking—but the key attraction was the reading. My aunt is long since dead, and of course I never told her. For that matter, maybe I never really sorted it out in my own mind, but there it was—no doubt about it.

As you might imagine, I wanted to go to school as soon as I could, and I made no secret about it. But you had to be six, and when they said six, they meant six. School started in September, but I was not six until November 13, 1932. So I was not allowed to begin until the next quarter—January 9, 1933.

My parents loaded me into a car (a new second hand Chevy bought especially for the occasion with hard earned savings) and took me to the residential school for the blind in Nashville fifty miles away. I entered the school grounds in early January of 1933 and didn't come out again until Easter when my parents took me home for the weekend.

That first year at the school for the blind in Nashville was quite an experience for me. I had never been away from my parents for any length of time in my whole life, and suddenly I was plopped down in the midst of twenty-five other small boys, who (though possessing certain cultural traits in common) came from widely diverse backgrounds and environments.

We called the woman who was in charge of us our supervisor. (We would have been outraged and humiliated by the term "house-mother.") She was a genteel person, the elderly widow of a doctor; and she did the best she could to teach us manners and morals, keep us in order, and raise us right.

But even if she had had the sleuthing skills of a Sherlock Holmes and the energy of a strong young athlete, she couldn't have kept track of us all of the time. Although we obeyed her rules and paid the penalty when we didn't—that is, when she caught us (I might say here that a heavy paddle was much in evidence), primarily we made our own rules and governed ourselves—at least in matters relating to social interaction.

One of the more noteworthy customs of the school was a Saturday morning ritual involving the Scriptures. Shortly after breakfast the small boys (I don't know what happened to the girls) were plopped down on a bench and given the task of memorizing a chapter from the Bible. It didn't do any good to protest, object, or try to resist. You sat there until you memorized it, after which you were free to go play.

One's religion had nothing to do with it, nor did one's interest or aptitude. When you got the task done, you could go where you pleased and do what you liked. Meanwhile, you couldn't. And any time you spent trying to beat the system was just that much of the morning gone.

I suppose I need not tell you that I quickly concluded to learn my chapter with minimum delay, which I religiously (no play on words intended) did. As a result, I have been a devout Bible quoter ever since—and much, I might add, to my benefit and long-range satisfaction. Ah, well, children are not always in the best position to know what will stand them in good stead.

At home on the farm my family got up early, often around four o'clock. My dad would go to the barn to feed the livestock and milk the cows, and my mother would build a fire in the wood stove and cook breakfast. We would then eat, and by the time it was light, my dad would be in the field to start his day's work. I got up when the others did, for the table was one place where I was equal with the rest. It was not just food that I got there but an important part of the day's routine and ritual—a time when all of us were together in a common activity.

But at school it was all different. I went to bed that first night at the school for the blind in a strange city and in the biggest building I had ever seen—a building with running water, indoor toilets, electricity, steam heat, and a group of strangers.

And as might have been predicted, I woke up about four o'clock the next morning. It was not only that I was wide awake and in a strange setting. I had to go to the bathroom (simply had to), and I didn't know where it was or how to get there. I didn't think I should wake anybody else up, but I knew I had to do something—so I got up, went out into the hall, and began to hunt.

Somehow (I don't know how I did it, but somehow) I found the bathroom, but then I didn't know how to get back to my room. At this point I simply lay down in the middle of the hall and waited for something to happen. It was an experience which I still vividly remember.

But that was not all that happened that day. When the other boys got up, I went with them to the bathroom to wash my hands and face and get ready for the day. One of them (he was nine and big for his age) said, "Here, give me your hand. I'll show you where to wash."

I wasn't very sophisticated, but it was clear he was trying to put my hand into the toilet. I was outraged. My mother and father didn't believe a blind person could do very much, and they had restricted my movements and actions—but they loved me, and even spoiled me. Certainly they never mistreated me.

My anger took tangible form. I jerked away and resisted, accompanying my actions with sharp words. The nine-year-old (who, as I was to learn, made a practice of bullying the smaller children) was not pleased to have his fun spoiled and to be resisted in the presence of the other boy. He beat me up. In fact, it was but the first of several beatings that he gave me during the next few days.

It was clear that I was either going to have to find a way to solve the problem or lead a life of intolerable misery. There were a number of other six- and seven-year-olds in the same boat. So I got together with them, and we went to see him as a group—and this time we didn't lose the fight. Just to make certain, we kept at it for a while until there was absolutely no doubt that we hadn't lost the fight. He never bothered us again.

It was my first lesson in the worthwhileness of collective action. It was a valuable learning experience, one that I have never forgotten. It has stood me in good stead through the years and been a comfort to me in times of trouble—and I am sure that it always will.

If I should ever be foolish enough to doubt the necessity of the National Federation of the Blind, all I would need to do would be to remember that week of misery in January of 1933 when I was six. That nine-year-old that I confronted may long since have passed to his reward, but he did me a service and taught me a lesson.

The most exciting thing about starting to school was finally learning to read. But I soon found that Braille was hard to come by at the Tennessee School for the Blind. As a matter of fact, it was <u>rationed</u>.

In the first grade we were allowed to read a book only during certain hours of the day, and we were not permitted to take books to our rooms at night or on weekends. Looking back, I suppose the school didn't have many books, and they probably thought (perhaps correctly) that those they did have would be used more as missiles than instruments of learning if they let us take them out.

When we advanced to the second grade, we were allowed (yes, allowed) to come down for thirty minutes each night to study hall. This was what the "big boys" did. In the first grade we had been ignominiously sent to bed at seven o'clock while our elders (the second and third graders and those beyond) were permitted to go to that mysterious place called study hall. The first graders (the "little boys") had no such status or privilege.

When we got to the third grade, we were still not permitted to take books to our rooms, but we were allowed to increase our study hall time. We could actually spend a whole hour at it each night Monday through Friday. It was the pinnacle of status for the primary grades.

When we got to the "intermediate" department (the fourth, fifth, and sixth grades) we were really "growing up," and our status and prestige increased accordingly. We were allowed (I use the word advisedly—"allowed," not "forced") to go for an hour each night Monday through Friday to study hall, and during that time we could read books and magazines to our hearts' content.

True, the choice was not great—but such as there was, we could read it. Of course, we could not take books to our rooms during the week, but on Friday night each boy (I presume the girls had the same privilege) could take one Braille volume to his room for the weekend.

Before I go further, perhaps I had better explain that comment about the girls. The girls sat on one side of the room, and the boys sat on the other; and woe to the member of one sex who tried to speak or write notes to a member of the other. Girls, like Braille books, were difficult to get at—and all the more desirable for the imagining. But back to the main thread.

As I say, each boy in the "intermediate" department could check out one Braille volume on Friday night. Now, as every good Braille reader knows, Braille is bulkier than print; and at least four or five Braille volumes (sometimes more) are required to make a book. It is also a matter of common knowledge that people in general and boys in particular (yes, and maybe girls, too) are constantly on the lookout for a way to "beat the system." What system? Any system.

So on Friday nights we boys formed what would today be called a consortium. One of us would check out volume one of a book; the next, volume two; the next, volume three; et cetera. With our treasures hugged to our bosoms we would head to our rooms and begin reading.

If you got volume three (the middle of the book), that's where you started. You would get to the beginning by and by. Now, girls and Braille books were not the only items that were strictly regulated in the environment I am describing. The hours of the day and night fell into the same category. Study hall ended at 8:00, and you were expected to be in your room and in bed by 9:40, the time when the "silence bell" rang. You were also expected to be trying to go to sleep, not reading.

But as I have said, people like to beat the system; and to us boys, starved for reading during the week, the hours between Friday night and Monday morning were not to be wasted. (Incidentally, I should say here that there were usually no radios around and that we were strictly forbidden—on pain of expulsion, and God knows what else—to leave the campus except for a brief period on Saturday afternoon—after we got big enough, that is, and assuming we had no violations on our record which required erasure by penalty.)

In other words the campus of the Tennessee School for the Blind was what one might call a closed ecology. We found our entertainment where we could.

Well, back to Friday night and the problem of books. Rules are rules, but Braille can be read under the covers as well as anywhere else; and when the lights are out and the sounds of approaching footsteps are easy to detect, it is virtually impossible to prohibit reading and make the prohibition stick.

The night watchman was regular in his rounds and methodical in his movements. He came through the halls every sixty minutes on the hour, and we could tell the time by his measured tread. (I suppose I need not add that we had no clocks or watches.)

After the watchman had left our vicinity, we would meet in the bathroom (there was one for all twenty-six of us) and discuss what we had been reading. We also used the occasion to keep ourselves awake and exchange Braille volumes as we finished them.

It made for an interesting way to read a book, but we got there—and instead of feeling deprived or abused, we felt elated. We were beating the system; we had books to read, something the little boys didn't have; and we were engaged in joint clandestine activity.

Sometimes as the night advanced, one of us would go to sleep and fail to keep the hourly rendezvous, but these were minor aberrations—and the weekend was only beginning.

After breakfast on Saturday morning some of us (not all) would continue reading—usually aloud in a group. We kept at it as long as we could, nodding off when we couldn't take it any more. Then, we went at it again.

Let me be clear. I am talking about a general pattern, not a rigid routine. It did not happen every weekend, and even when it did, the pace was not uniform or the schedule precise. We took time for such pleasantries as running, playing, and occasional rock fights.

You can understand that after I had been in school for a few weeks, I contemplated with mixed feelings the summer vacation which would be coming. I loved my family, but I had been away from home and found stimulation and new experiences. I did not look forward to three months of renewed confinement in the four-room farm house with nothing to do.

Then, I learned that I was going to be sent a Braille magazine during the summer months. Each month's issue was sixty Braille pages. I would get one in June, one in July, and one in August. What joy! I was six, but I had learned what boredom meant—and I had also learned to plan. So I rationed the Braille and read two pages each day. This gave me something new for tomorrow. Of course, I went back and read and re-read it again, but the two new pages were always there for tomorrow.

As the school years came and went, I got other magazines, learned about the Library of Congress Braille and talking book collection, and got a talking book machine. By the time I was in the seventh grade I was receiving a number of Braille magazines and ordering books from three separate libraries during the summer. Often I would read twenty hours a day—not every day, of course, but often. I read Gone With the Wind, War and Peace, Zane Grey, and hundreds of others.

I read whatever the libraries sent me, every word of it; and I often took notes. By then it was clear to me that books would be my release from the prison of the farm and inactivity. It was also clear to me that college was part of that program and that somehow I was going to get there. But it was not just escape from confinement or hope for a broader horizon or something to be gained. It was also a deep, ingrained love of reading.

The background I have described conditioned me. I did not feel about reading the way I see a lot of people viewing it today. Many of today's children seem to have the attitude that they are "forced," not "permitted," to go to school—that they are "required," not "given the privilege and honor," to study.

They are inundated with reading matter. It is not scarce but a veritable clutter, not something to strive for but to take for granted. I don't want children or the general public to be deprived of reading matter, but I sometimes think that a scald is as bad as a freeze. Is it worse to be deprived of books until you feel starved for them or to be so overwhelmed with them that you become blase about it? I don't know, and I don't know that it will do me any good to speculate.

All I know is that I not only delight in reading but believe it to be a much neglected joy and a principal passport to success, perspective, civilization, and possibly the survival of the species. I am extremely glad I have had the opportunity and incentive to read as broadly as I have, and I believe my life is so much better for the experience that it borders on the difference between living and existence.

The world today is much different for everyone from what it was when I was a child. And for blind people it is a better world with more opportunities and a better future ahead because we have worked with each other and with generous and caring sighted people to make it so. I believe there are few problems in life that can't be solved when people do what they can for themselves and join together to help others. I am grateful for the help I have received in my lifetime and try to do my share to make the world a better place for all of us.

THE ENCHANTED KINGDOM: REFLECTIONS ON THE TALKING BOOK

by Barbara Pierce

As the poet Robert Service said, there is a hunger "not of the belly kind that's filled with bacon and beans." There is the hunger of a blind child who wants contact with the world around her. Barbara Pierce is the wife of a college professor, the mother of three well-adjusted intelligent children in young adulthood, and the President of the National Federation of the Blind of Ohio. She has worked as the assistant alumni director of Oberlin College—but it was not always like that. She remembers.

When I was nine, my father walked in from work one day carrying a large, heavy case. My brother and I were consumed with curiosity, and my smugness and self-importance knew no bounds when he explained that the box was for me. Nothing, however, could have prepared me for the revolution that the heavy gray case would create in my life.

The year was 1954, and the box was a Talking Book record player from the Library of Congress. If the President himself had presented me with the machine, I could not have been more astonished. I now know that, two years before, Congress had amended the Pratt-Smoot Act to include children in the Talking Book Program.

But as I remember the lecture I was given that day, special arrangements had been made [I was certain that these had been at the highest levels of government], and it had been decided to allow me to read books on records because everyone knew what a careful and responsible girl I was. If I failed to operate the machine properly or (inconceivable catastrophe) if I broke one of the records, no other child would ever be given the privilege that I now saw shimmering on my horizon.

The record player was set up in the downstairs bedroom, and I began to read. "The Privateer" by Gordon Daviot, "Little Men" by Louisa May Alcott, and "Bless This House" by Norah Lofts: these were the first three books. I promised myself that I would memorize the author of every book I read and the order in which I had consumed their work. I did pretty well at it for the first twenty books or so, but then I began to understand just how many books a person really could read, and my good intentions dissolved.

Within a week the Talking Book machine was moved to my room so that the rest of the family didn't have to listen along with me. My bedroom never had much heat, and that winter I could only keep my hands warm by holding them over the glowing red light that indicated that the machine motor was turned on. I was lucky that those record players in the fifties threw out so much heat; otherwise frost bite would have found a contented victim.

Until that intoxicating day when the Talking Book program walked into my life, I had had two choices when I wanted or needed to read a book. First, I could don a pair of heavy glasses with tremendous magnification in one lens; hunch over the page of print in very bright light; and struggle letter by letter to decipher the text, praying the while for a picture or, better yet, lots of pictures to take up space.

My other alternative was to lie in wait for a member of my family. My brother, seven at the time, was good for comic books and not much more. Unfortunately, he favored Superman, and I preferred Scrooge McDuck. His verbal skills were taxed acutely by describing the pictures, and altogether Bobby was less satisfactory than my parents, if I could get them.

I had already read "Heidi" and "Charlotte's Web" in ten-minute snatches, my mother's method of bribing me to do wretched eye exercises every day. My parents were generous with their time, but they were already helping me with every bit of my considerable homework, and there were limits to what even I was prepared to request. So the Talking Book machine and those amazing twelve-inch records played at 33 1/3 rpm really did change my life.

I became the envy of my classmates. Not held down by such annoyances as vocabulary and spelling, I sailed into uncharted waters beyond my years. Teachers could easily be dazzled by book reports on the works of Dickens, Hawthorne, and Dostoyevsky. There were also those occasional passages which I found very illuminating but which I knew instinctively my parents had much better not overhear.

I know now that, had Braille been offered me in these formative years, I would today be a much better educated person, but it was to be another twenty years before I heard of the National Federation of the Blind, and there was no one in my life warning me that Braille was essential to my education.

Proud mother, Ramona Walhof, with her now grown children—Laura, a senior at M.I.T., and Christopher, a sophomore at the University of Idaho. They didn't get corrupted.

I AM A BLIND MOTHER FIGHTING TO KEEP MY CHILDREN FROM CORRUPTION

by Ramona Walhof

Ramona Walhof is the President of the National Federation of the Blind of Idaho. She gives her time to the Federation because of the fight she had to make to keep her children from being destroyed.

I am blind, and I have two sighted children. When they started school, I found it necessary to work hard to guard them against corruption. I am not talking about drugs, vulgar language, crime, or any of the things with which all families must cope. My children faced a very special, if unintentional, kind of corruption.

It never occurred to my husband and me that blindness could be considered a reason not to have children. We were both blind. We considered blindness a nuisance, but it didn't prevent us from living active and productive lives. We both had college degrees and good jobs.

My husband was a rehabilitation counselor for the Idaho Commission for the Blind. I was teaching in the Head Start program. My class consisted of 15 four-year-olds from deprived families. The real problem of blindness was that sighted people much too often treated us as if we had no ability, intelligence, or skills.

After we were married, we worked hard to save enough money for the down payment on a house. We found one we could afford on a bus line in North Boise. It was old-fashioned and comfortable, and we bought it.

When we discovered that I was pregnant, we were delighted. Both sets of grandparents-to-be were also thrilled. We learned that when parents become grandparents, they are able to relax and enjoy the children. They are not expected to do the discipline. It must not have occurred to any of them that blindness could be considered a reason not to have children. But then they knew us pretty well, and they had learned some things about blindness as we learned them.

We bought a crib and borrowed a basket. I bought diapers, undershirts, baby blankets, and the like. I got out the sewing machine to make maternity clothes. We were still budgeting carefully. That session of Head Start ended in May when the school year ended, and we still had a month to wait for the baby. It was the longest month of my life.

My husband and I always made plans to attend the conventions of the National Federation of the Blind over the Fourth of July weekend, but that year we stayed home. Our friends went camping, fishing, waterskiing, etc., and we read books at home.

Finally, on July 9, Laura Kathyrn decided to enter the big, wide world, and she didn't waste any time once she started. We arrived at the hospital at 9:35 a.m., and Laura arrived at 10:13 a.m. My husband didn't complain about not getting the boy he wanted. He was extremely proud. I was feeling fine, and it became almost a race to see which of us could reach our friends first to tell them the baby had finally arrived.

The hospital where Laura was born had a practice of having new mothers assist with the bathing of the baby at least once before taking it home from the hospital. I had changed diapers and given bottles many times, but I had very little experience with a baby that weighed 7 pounds, so I was eager for some suggestions.

I was lucky that the nurse involved did not get upset about the blindness. She just told me what to do, and I did it. Seldom since then has anyone been so matter-of-fact, and I appreciated it. Sight, as I expected, was not necessary. Babies are fragile and delicate, but they want and need to be touched.

After Laura and I came home from the hospital, my mother came from Nebraska to stay with us for a week. She was truly helpful. She did the housework and most of the cooking and left the baby care to me. From her own experiences she came up with some suggestions I found useful. By the end of the week I had most of my energy back, and Grandma went back to Nebraska.

Laura was a pretty baby, healthy and alert. She obviously was not blind. She responded to color and movement when only a few days old. We spent a few nights up— baby screaming with a tummy ache. For the most part, however, everything continued to go smoothly.

By the time Laura was 3 months old, I began to grow restless. I wasn't used to staying home all day, even with a baby for company. Sometimes my husband had to be out of town for several days at a time in his work, so I began to look for some other things to do.

Head Start was beginning a new program in November, so I applied for a teaching job. When I got the job, we started looking for a baby-sitter. We were happy to find a good one.

By Christmas Laura was crawling and pulling herself up on her feet. I have a picture taken of her at Christmas time crawling into the dishwasher. She had become quite a flirt by then also. She squealed at her daddy and played peekaboo with her grandpa.

We knew that if we were to use a baby buggy or stroller we would need to pull it behind us, using the white cane in the other hand in front for safety. We found a buggy that converted into a stroller. This met the need, and we used it a great deal. It even folded up, so we could take it on the city buses.

With a little practice we also became proficient at carrying Laura in an infant seat balanced on both forearms and one hand. We could dangle the diaper bag from an elbow, leaving the other hand free to use the white cane.

Since Laura stayed with a baby-sitter during the day while I worked, I took her with me as much as I could. She seemed to like people; and I suppose what pleased me most was that people everywhere admired her.

By Mother's Day Laura was walking. My father-in-law took us all out to eat, and here was Laura all dressed up in yellow and white, toddling around awkwardly and with a smile for everyone. My first Mother's Day was very special. For both my husband and me, it was a day we would always remember as ours.

In July of that year my husband and I did get to go to the convention of the National Federation of the Blind, which was in Houston, Texas. Laura celebrated her first birthday at her Grandparents' house in Nebraska. When we returned there from the convention, she was thrilled to see her daddy, but mother was ignored. However, by the time the birthday cake appeared, she had hugs and kisses for me, too.

We were expecting another child in the fall. My husband still wanted a boy, and I thought two children close together in age would entertain each other. They did and they do. They also fight.

I had been managing a cafeteria during the summer, and I quit in September to do some work at home before the new baby arrived. Among other things I wallpapered the kids' bedroom with a nursery print. Laura loved it. She would point to the various animals and figures happily. Gradually she learned to say their names.

She would take guests by a finger and lead them upstairs to show them her pretty wallpaper with pictures. She had been eating with a spoon since about 13 months. I didn't let her pick up food out of her plate with her hands, so she really wasn't as messy an eater as some small children just learning.

Our little boy was born on December 20, and we named him Christopher John. Chris was healthy, alert, cuddly, and always hungry. One evening just before we took Chris home from the hospital, one of the nurses stood watching me feeding him and commented, "You handle him so well." I knew she meant that since I was blind this surprised her, but I only smiled at her and asked if she worked in the nursery. She said she did and added, "We had a blind woman in here a while ago who couldn't get her baby to nurse very well." So I knew there was more involved than the usual lack of knowledge about blindness. I figured that blindness had nothing to do with whether a mother had trouble getting her baby to nurse or not. I have several sighted friends who had trouble at first.

"That's interesting," I said. "I've known several people who had trouble getting started, but none of them were blind." Of course the nurse wasn't convinced. She gave me enough information that I realized I knew the woman she had mentioned. Her baby was about six months old by this time, still breast-feeding and doing fine. The trouble must have been very minor, because my friend had never mentioned it.

I took note of an example of people attributing every problem a blind person has to the blindness. It just didn't seem fair. If my kids ever got hurt (and all kids do), would people blame me? I was forced to conclude that many would.

Chris and I went home from the hospital the day before Christmas. Luckily all the shopping was done, and most of the presents were wrapped. My mother-in-law had invited us to their home for Christmas dinner, and I was glad to take it easy.

That Christmas Laura was the center of attention and was enjoying herself. She wanted to share everything with her baby brother whether he cared or not. In a way she thought he was one of her Christmas presents, although we had been waiting even longer for his arrival than for Christmas.

I could put Chris in the infant seat in the stroller with Laura beside him, and we could take short trips like that. There wasn't much snow that year in Boise; so often when we went out, Laura could walk. I could let her walk only if we weren't in a hurry, for she made lots of detours off the main sidewalk, and I would have to stop and wait for her or bring her back. My husband was glad to have a little boy, but his daughter was really his pride and joy.

Shortly after we brought Chris home from the hospital, my husband began to have problems with his health. We saw a specialist who told us the condition would become stable with medication, but that didn't happen.

I was glad both children were healthy, but I didn't have time to consider going back to work myself. My husband was in and out of the hospital for the next couple of months, and in April he died. It was a hard winter and spring.

Laura insisted on having some explanations, and I did my best to help her understand. Her daddy had come home from the hospital many times; and no matter how he felt, he always had a smile and a hug for Laura. She could not believe she could not see him anymore.

It was hard enough for me to accept the whole thing. How could I explain it to a child 21 months old and help her to accept it? But I had to go on. I had two babies depending on me, and I would not let them down if I could help it.

Before my marriage I had worked as a teacher for the Iowa Commission for the Blind. My employer had been Dr. Kenneth Jernigan, who was also President of the National Federation of the Blind, the organization to which we belonged and which was changing so many things for the blind in the 1960s and 1970s.

I turned to Dr. Jernigan, hoping I again could find employment at the Iowa Commission. The jobs I had held in Boise hadn't paid enough money to support a family now that there was just one salary. Dr. Jernigan told me there would be an opening at the Commission in June. I thought I could be ready.

I put our house in Boise up for sale, and it sold. We moved into an apartment in Des Moines, Iowa. A cousin of mine who was in high school came to stay with us for the summer until I could find a regular baby-sitter. I was ready to go to work by the second week in June.

The new job was a demanding one and a rewarding one. We settled in and started over. By October I had found a house and made the down payment. It had three bedrooms and a nice backyard. The day we moved into our new home, Christopher started to walk. He had been slow to roll over, sit up, and crawl, but not to walk.

Our new home had all hardwood floors. His little shoes got good traction, and he had a whole house to explore. He didn't sit down all day long, except for a nap. By the end of the day he was running. I had planned to let him stay in the playpen while I unpacked.

That was one of those plans that get rejected by the next generation. He enjoyed walking so much, and he had so much space in the new house to investigate, I just didn't have the heart to coop him up in the playpen.

As might be expected, Chris's character was entirely different from Laura's. He could then and still can be very demanding. Laura got attention, for the most part, with smiles and flirtation. Chris knew how to do that, but he also made use of tantrums from time to time. Laura wanted to be where I was as much as possible. Chris, even when he was tiny, did not mind playing by himself for an hour at a time.

When the weather turned nice in the spring, Chris was curious to explore the neighborhood. I could count on Laura to stay in the backyard, but not Christopher! When he went outside that year, Mother went along.

One day he climbed to the top of the iron grillwork on our front stoop. He couldn't get down, and I couldn't reach him. I said nothing, but went into the house to get a chair to climb up and get him. He wasn't frightened, but I was glad to have him back on the ground.

I suppose Chris was too busy to talk much that summer. Only occasionally a word slipped out. Sometime in October—all of a sudden, just the way he learned to walk—he started talking. And he talked all the time. And then the questions began. Laura had been asking some questions, of course. But Christopher wanted to know everything: "Why, Mommy? When? How?"

By this time both children liked books. My baby-sitter read to them during the day, and I read to them at bedtime. I was able to borrow books for small children from the Iowa Commission for the Blind.

The books had the text and pictures in both Braille and print. These are known as Twin-Vision books and are produced by the American Brotherhood for the Blind. I read with my fingers; others read with their eyes. My children grew up finding this quite natural and uninteresting.

By the time Laura was four, she began to ask, "When can I go to school, Mommy?" There were no children her age in the neighborhood, but she played with the children of friends. She knew the alphabet and numbers and had known them since the age of two.

Laura was a quiet child and sometimes a little overwhelmed by crowds, but if she found kindergarten frightening, she never let me know. She made many new friends; and for her, that was the best part of starting school.

Both children when tiny had accepted my blindness as normal and okay. I carried a white cane and used it to find steps, curbs, and other obstacles when we went away from home. We rode on buses and in taxicabs more than some people, because I did not drive a car. I read Braille with my fingers, while others read print with their eyes. That's about all there was to it.

If the children had a toy to be fixed or a question to be answered, I was the first person they asked to do it. Sometimes I couldn't or wouldn't do what they asked, but most of the time I could and did.

When Laura started to school, she began to hear some different things about blindness. I can only guess what happened. Someone must have said to her, "I bet you're a big help to your mommy, aren't you?"

At first she must have smiled and nodded proudly. Then she began to understand they were saying that something about her mommy was different. Someone must have pointed her out on the playground and said in a whisper, "That little girl's mother is blind." And soon I became aware of a change in her attitude toward blindness.

One day when Laura was helping me find a spool of red thread in the sewing machine drawer, she said to me, "Mommy, I wish you could see."

"Well, so do I, if I ever think about it," I answered. "But why do you bring it up?"

"Well—" She couldn't quite find the words to say what she meant. "Well, then I might not have to help you so much."

I began to understand what was happening to her. I thought a minute; then I took her on my lap.

"I have some Braille labels for the thread and for the cans of fruit and vegetables in the kitchen," I told her. "We can put them on, and then you won't have to help me with those things anymore." Chris and Laura regarded it as a real privilege to choose fruit or vegetables for dinner, so she didn't like that idea very much. Laura was a little confused.

"I just wish you could see like other people," she said. It had never bothered her before, so something or someone at school, it seemed to me, must have made Laura think blindness was a problem. I gave her a hug and told her not to worry about it.

"You know better than most people," I said, "that blindness isn't really as big a problem as people think it is." I knew, though, that I needed to get busy and help the people at school learn some things about blindness.

The PTA scheduled an ice cream social in October. I baked brownies for it, and we went. When we walked in the door, no one knew what to do. One woman tried to drag us through a line backwards. Another was so worried about how we would get our ice cream and cake that we could hardly get her to sell us tickets. Others ignored us completely when we tried to get directions. I felt like a ghost or a body from outer space.

No one was able to converse with me like a normal human being. But we did get our ice cream and cake. We sat down and ate them and left. I knew I must do more than that if my children's attitudes about blindness were not to be totally ruined.

At the end of the first quarter, parents go to the school for conferences. Laura's teacher said my daughter was doing fine—there were no problems in school. The teacher was a little uneasy about the blindness, so I asked her if she would like me to come and talk to the class about Braille and blindness sometime.

This pleased the teacher, and she also wanted Laura to bring a book with Braille in it that she could show to the class. This, I thought, would help Laura understand that people who know little or nothing about blindness are curious. It did.

By the time I actually went to the school to talk, the project had broadened, and I was to speak to the entire school, two grades at a time. The students loved it and had lots of questions—things their teachers would have been embarrassed to ask. "Why do your eyes wiggle?" "Do you have school books in Braille?" "How do you get to work?" I assumed the teachers were listening, and I told the kids what I wanted them and their teachers to know.

I told them, for instance, that the fact that I and others are blind is not a big problem, that the problems we face are a result of the fact that so many people who can see think blind people cannot do all of the things that we really can do.

It made good sense to the kids, as is often the case. It helped the teachers also, and they were genuine in their thanks for a presentation that was helpful to the kids.

Since then I have been to the school many times. I am much better acquainted with the teachers and parents and many of the kids. Many of them think of me as the blind lady, but they don't worry about it.

We have had birthday parties and Easter egg hunts at our house. I have helped with Laura's Blue Bird Club, and we had a club meeting at our house. Kids float in and out regularly, especially when the weather is nice.

Chris is now in kindergarten, and Laura is in second grade. Some things are very much different. After the first few weeks of school, Chris came home and told me, "My teacher says I can bring a Braille book to school tomorrow if I want to." This is the same teacher who taught Laura in Kindergarten. Chris was pleased to be asked to do that.

Somehow, the whole neighborhood seems more friendly.

I have always tried to teach my children to respect their teachers and baby-sitters.

Now I must teach them that, at least with respect to blindness, they have more knowledge and experience than many adults they will meet. It is risky to tell children that is so about anything at such a young age. Yet it is important to me and to them that their thinking about blindness remain what it is.

Laura helps me with the grocery shopping, just as she helps clean up her room. Chris helps take care of the dog, just as he helps sort socks in the laundry. Blindness is a characteristic. It is not to be forgotten or ignored, but it is only a characteristic.

Mothers make their kids keep dirt outdoors (if they can). Mothers prepare meals. Mothers don't like kids to fight. Mothers sometimes have money kids can help spend. Sometimes mothers make rules kids don't like. Sometimes mothers help make kids feel better when they have a problem. Blind mothers are like other mothers. My kids know it, and their friends know it.

WHAT COLOR IS THE SUN

by Lauren L. Eckery

Lauren Eckery and her daughter Lynden are well known to the members of the National Federation of the Blind throughout the country. The Eckery's (Laurie and Jerry) are both blind. Their daughter Lynden is not. Lynden is a normal, bright, sensitive little girl, curious about the world around her. Laurie and Jerry are also normal, bright, and sensitive. Blindness is simply one of their many traits. Their experiences with their sighted daughter not only touch the heart but also give us a realistic picture of what blindness is like in daily life.

The burning hot sun of midsummer is shining brightly today as I sit out here on the patio beginning to write. What "color" the sun is is not particularly relevant to me at this moment. I know that for some blind people the color of the sun or, for that matter, what anything looks like visually, seems irrelevant. I do not take this view, however. I am highly interested in my world, including what things look like. There are those who might insist that this could not be so.

Back in 1972, when I was nearing graduation from the University of Nebraska at Lincoln, a sighted male friend and I were discussing my future. This was a friend I very much liked and trusted.

Neither of us understood what he was really saying when he remarked: "When you get an apartment of your own, if you have cockroaches, they won't bother you because you won't see them, so you won't even know they are there. Besides, if you don't know what they look like, then you won't know how awful they are."

As Pearl S. Buck has written: "There were many ways of breaking a heart. Stories were full of hearts being broken by love, but what really broke a heart was taking away its dream—whatever that dream might be."

My dream, of course, was to be a normal, first-class citizen in our society. My dream, at that particular time, might have included him in that apartment of the future. He had obviously highly respected me as a student, equal to himself, but he really did not respect me as a blind person.

Evidently he assumed that a blind person keeping an apartment by him- or herself would necessarily have cockroaches, since blind people couldn't possibly keep the place clean. (I may not be the best housekeeper, but blindness is not the reason.)

How misinformed was this fine young man, even though he had known me for several years. How misinformed was I to the extent that I was unable to set him straight about blindness, resulting in discouraging him from remaining in a prominent place in my life.

But all of this was twenty years ago before I found the National Federation of the Blind. How differently I would react today. As I began to grow in the Federation, I learned from those who were willing to teach me, and I have also learned from experience (sometimes the hard way) some of the realities of blindness—mainly attitude problems and their impact on our lives and the means for solving such problems.

Shared individual positive experiences can help us learn to believe in ourselves. This is what the National Federation of the Blind is truly all about. To this end I relate the following experience: Several weeks ago my eight-year-old daughter, Lynden, asked:

"Mommy, what color is the sun?" She blinks and often sneezes upon looking directly at the sun. Was it possible that she never looked long enough to notice the color of the sun? Was she testing me to see if I knew the color of the sun? What answer did she expect to get from me, the standard "yellow"?

I am totally blind since birth due to congenital glaucoma. I have no vision in the left eye. Before glaucoma took my right eye, I could see light, dark, and blobs of color. I cried the evening before the surgery, panicked a few times immediately thereafter, and that was it.

I was not bitter about never seeing another sunset, because I knew that in my mind's eye I could conjure one up easily enough if I wanted to do so. Perhaps this is similar to the manner in which Beethoven was able to write some of his best music when he could no longer hear—he had a good mind, and he used it.

I told Lynden that in the middle of the day the sun is said to be yellow, although it always looked white to me. I explained that toward sunset the color could change from a brighter yellow, becoming more and more orange, sometimes setting in a brilliant red-orange ball with other colors around it (clouds, I surmised).

When this occurs, the bright fiery ball on the horizon looks as though it is resting on the ground, quite far away. Eventually it disappears. Sometimes the clouds hide this color. Often the sun does just the opposite at sunrise.

Sunrises and sunsets can vary. Artists have painted them; writers have described them in words. Some people often do not notice them at all, but they are there.

"I've never seen the sun change color like that. Why does it change color? Why does it look like the sun is on the ground?" she asked, curiously. Her questions were getting beyond me. I didn't know enough about the physical properties of light, color, refraction, and distance, plus the rotation of the earth, etc., to explain it all to her. Anxiously I said: "Ask your science teacher when school starts again."

With a sigh of relief, I presumed the subject closed, only to hear: "Mommy, could you see rays coming out of the sun?" I told her I couldn't.

"Me neither," she replied. "Then why do people make pictures of the sun with rays coming out all around it?" she continued.

I thought: "Ask your art teacher when school starts again." However, being somewhat more artistic than scientific, I explained that maybe it was an artistic way to show that light and heat were coming from all directions from the yellow circle which represented the sun in the pictures. That was the end of the discussion for the time being.

I believe that Lynden was surprised by the answer she got from a totally blind person. I was equally astonished that a sighted child would bother to ask a totally blind person to describe something visual, taking the answer seriously. I believe we both learned something extremely valuable from this experience.

The knowledge gained and the joy received from this experience were made evident this past weekend as we were riding the bus home from Kansas City to Omaha. Lynden had been sleeping, and I was listening to my tape recorder. Suddenly she shouted, with obvious delight, "Mommy, the sun is orange and it is on the ground just like you said." (It looked like it was on the ground.) "It is red-orange, and it's pretty. I've never seen that before."

I was aware that if I had believed all of the stereotypes about blindness, that I would never have done such a normal thing as to get married and have a child—one I was now sharing a sunset with—because I might have believed that a blind person couldn't take care of a child independently. I was thankful for this National Federation of the Blind-influenced blessing.

I was also aware at that moment that this sunset might have gone unnoticed by both of us had we not had our previous discussion. Certainly it would not have been a life-or-death disaster to have missed the sunset, but there was a particular joy in our sharing, "What color is the sun?"

Having grown up on a farm, Bill is an enthusiastic gardener. He follows his rows using string markers.

LET THE FLAG SPEAK

by Bill J. Isaacs

Bill Isaacs grew up on a farm as a member of a large family. He likes to garden, and he takes seriously the notion of freedom—and also of responsibility. He is a teacher, the kind of person you would like for a friend or neighbor. He is one of the leaders of the National Federation of the Blind of Illinois.

It is rather ironic that on the same day the Supreme Court in defense of freedom of expression struck down a state law protecting the flag from desecration, a lower magistrate fined a fellow for noise pollution because his boisterous, vibrating flag annoyed his neighbors. As it were, in the latter instance, it was illegal for the rippling flag to speak to the breezes. Allowing the flag to speak for itself brings back nostalgic memories.

Except for three years of graduate study at the University of Illinois, I have been part of the Olivet Nazarene University academic community as a student or faculty member since 1954. Up until about five years ago there was an ever-waving flag positioned on the highest knoll on campus about 150 feet in front of the Administration Building, where my office and classroom are located on the third floor.

Whether in the office or walking across campus, I could nearly always hear the flag bracing itself against the wind. I most certainly never considered it to be an annoyance but very much a friendly chatter. If I strayed too much with my white cane or gave my guide dog wrong directions because of a blanket of snow, a welcome ripple of the flag always gave me the feeling that I was not completely lost and could always work my way back toward it.

This dependable flag communicated with me. It spoke to me in countless ways. Its musical rhythm sang to me: "The Star-Spangled Banner," "America the Beautiful," "This Land is Your Land, This Land is My Land," etc. Oftentimes I found myself marching to its rhythm. In some ways the messages the flag shared with me remind me of the unspoken body language that my dog and I daily share with each other. In the case of the flag, however, it was perhaps more a one-way signal rather than a reciprocal one.

You can understand, I think, why after thirty years I miss this compass point, "Old

Glory" when she was hauled down in deference to the much lower, multi-flag display arranged at the new entrance of University Avenue (old Olivet Street). I am sure the new display is beautiful, but beauty lies in the eye of the beholder.

The beholding, for some like myself, lies in the hearing of the ear, the taste of the tongue, or the touch of the hand. According to the English poet Keats, "A thing of beauty is a joy forever." Beauty can be experienced through all the senses. Furthermore, I had to replace my first guide dog about the same time the flag was removed. It was a lot like losing two close companions simultaneously. That certain joy, that rhythmic feeling had been muzzled.

When I began to make inquiry from my colleagues who were as ill-informed as I about the flag's removal, they had to take a look to see if it were truly gone. It was then I began to realize that the flag probably meant more to me than to any other person. Probably, like Thoreau, I was marching to the beat of a different drummer.

Supposedly one glimpse of the American flag by the light of an exploding bomb inspired Francis Scott Key to pour forth the words of the National Anthem as he viewed it from a British prison ship. I still find my-self, five years later, listening for the sound of the musical flag.

About a year ago the old flag pole was sawed to pieces and the cement base was broken up and carried away. Grave-like sod now covers the ground where my messenger friend stood. Though dismantled, muted, and uprooted, in my heart and in my mind's eye I still hear the faint echoes of the speaking flag!

BLIND FAITH

by Mike Pearson

This perceptive and sensitive story first appeared in the Rocky Mountain News. *It was later reprinted in the* Braille Monitor, *the publication of the National Federation of the Blind. It appears here because it does more than tell the particular events of a physical challenge. It symbolizes hope, belief, and the courage to dream.*

Faith and fear are fraternal twins born a heartbeat apart.

On a cold May morning at the tail end of sunrise, the twins lie in wait in a canyon in Eldorado Springs. They watch silently as a group of seven students disembark a bus and prepare for their first climb up a jagged rock wall.

Muscular, cheerful instructors from the International Alpine School scurry around untangling ropes, threading harnesses, handing out soft-soled shoes. The students are a bit more tentative in their enthusiasm. The scent of a challenge hangs heavy in the air, and casual conversation masks their apprehension.

The idea of scrambling up the face of a 200-foot-high rock would take most mortals aback. Falling is not a pleasant concept. But these mortals, armed with backpacks and water bottles and guts, are more extraordinary than most.

They're from the National Federation of the Blind's Colorado Center for the Blind in Denver, and on this morning they will defy the conventional wisdom of the sighted and stalk the mountain sky.

As instructors make last-minute adjustments to equipment and brief their charges on the quarter-mile hike up the canyon, Diane McGeorge stands off to one side smiling as though she has just won an Academy Award. As director of the Center for the Blind, McGeorge has accompanied two previous groups of students through the six-week program. She is a veteran mountain tamer, no less fierce for her lack of sight, with unshakable praise for the program.

"This has really been great for our students," she says, a hint of anticipation in her voice. "One of the neatest things it's done for blind students is challenge their self-discipline. Sure, the students are worried. All of us come here with a lot of fear and a lot of misgivings."

He climbs rocks to a new life.

"But perhaps the most important part of the program is that it teaches us that we can reach way down inside and do a lot of the things we didn't think we could do. We can overcome our fears—physical, mental, and emotional."

"One of the most common things I hear people say is, 'It's probably easier for you because you don't have to worry about the fear of looking down.' I tell them everybody has fears, and it doesn't have anything to do with being blind."

"If you're climbing and you realize, 'My God, I'm 100 feet in the air,' or you hear the river rushing way down below, you really learn the meaning of trust. But fear is inside you all the time. And you have to conquer that fear every day."

The sun has finally burned off the morning mist as the caravan starts down the trail into the canyon. The students can't see the sheer beauty of their surroundings, the angry curve of the rock, the sliver of sky that forms a canopy as they hike farther along the trail.

But they can hear and smell and touch the world around them. The chatter of birds, the thrashing of a swollen stream are as vivid as any colors known to man. As the wind brushes by with a soothing sigh, they know the adventure has just begun.

Students at the Colorado Center for the Blind learn to read Braille, they learn how to travel independently, cook for themselves, and live on their own. And they learn to climb rocks.

Homer Page, Chairman of the Center's Board, believes rock climbing forces blind students to confront their fears.

"Some of them never do like it, whereas others want to continue climbing for years," he said. "You can tell people that blind people aren't limited by lack of sight, and it goes in one ear and out the other. It's just not the same as going out and tackling a tough physical challenge. We want them to come away with a feeling that they can do many things they never imagined. They don't have to quit. They don't have to be afraid of life."

It's high noon on a sweltering June day in Gregory Canyon on the outskirts of Boulder. The sun bleeds sweat from the pale pink rock, banishing shadows to the safety of an occasional crack. This is the fabled amphitheater, where the last class of each session takes place.

And today is graduation day.

The objective is for students to top-rope it up this unforgiving rock and rappel back down. By this final day, the instructor's primary role is to offer encouragement from below. It will be a test of blind faith. Courage and commitment.

Yet, unlike the first day of class, when anxiety was the prevalent emotion, today the talk is boisterous, the laughter common, and the energy level high.

For 40-year-old James Wolcott, the six-week span has brought a big change.

"This is the first time I've ever taken a class like this, and I think it's great," he said, lightly stepping over a carpet of broken rocks. "It's definitely been a challenge. The hardest part has been forcing myself beyond what I thought I could do. Society probably doesn't understand what we're doing here. They probably don't think something like this is possible, but I know it's very possible. I'm scared every time I climb up there. But afterward I feel really great."

For group leader Joanne Yankovich, who has been leading the class since its inception, such an endorsement makes the long hours and tiring regimen—including a couple of 3-mile "death marches" to condition the students—worthwhile.

"The funny thing is how much I learn about myself through this class," she said, securing a top rope for the first of the students. "The climbing issues are the same as any other class—fear, athletic self-doubt, and learning to trust your equipment and your partner.

But the fact that these are people who don't have sight brings up special issues, especially social stereotypes about what they can or can't do. Whenever I tell sighted people about this class, they're surprised. They've just never considered a blind person's being able to climb a rock, or even wanting to."

"Of course, the school's main objective is mobility. If they can get through this, it gives them a lot of confidence to try other things. This is probably the most complicated set of mobility problems you can give anybody, blind or sighted. I mean, in an urban environment everything is normally square or rectangular. When you're climbing a rock wall, a cane isn't of much use."

Every challenge provides an opportunity for growth.

"It's about assuming responsibility for one's self in an age when people are more and more willing to abdicate that," she said. "Yes, there is risk involved. But it's like anything else: if you want to test your limits it can be hard. But ultimately, it is also rewarding."

One student summed it up: "If you can climb a rock, crossing Broadway and Evans in Denver isn't so scary," he said. "Something like this gives you a sense of perspective."

HOMEMAKING AFTER I BECAME BLIND

by Mary Lou Hentges

Until her recent death, Mary Lou Hentges was an active member of the National Federation of the Blind. She and her husband Clete traveled widely, spreading the hope and courage they found in the National Federation of the Blind.

I became blind just when my children were finishing school and my husband was ready to retire. At first it seemed as though blindness would ruin all our plans and dreams. But it didn't work out that way at all.

I found that blind people use their other senses to help them when the vision is gone. I listen for cars before crossing the street. I find that I hear many more things than my husband does. That's because I have learned to use my ears. My hands can tell me a lot too. Touch is something I learned to use.

I have learned that I can smell when the chicken or other things that I am frying need to be turned over. The sound of the sizzle and smell tell me. All of these things sound almost impossible, I know, but after awhile they came to me naturally. If I become frustrated trying to do something, I just quit, walk away from it and come back to it later.

I have a talking clock. It gives the time each hour and has a button to press to get the time during the hour. I have a small one that I carry in my purse. I also have a talking alarm clock in the bedroom.

I put a mark on the dial of my washing machine and dryer. This is marked on the setting that I use the most; the dryer is marked at thirty minutes. I have an iron that I can tell where the setting for cotton is. You can buy irons that click at each setting.

I have my electric skillets, deep fryer and oven marked at three hundred degrees and then I can judge if I need a hotter or cooler temperature for each.

I have the thermostat for the furnace marked at seventy degrees and can lower or raise the temperature.

There is a marking glue that can be bought at any good hardware store made especially for this purpose. My husband used a small piece of a flat toothpick and glued it to the dial for my washer and dryer. This works well for me.

When baking, I pull the rack out of the oven several inches and then put my finger on the top of the cookies to see if they are done. You may burn your fingers at first, but you will soon learn to feel the heat and can tell where to put your finger.

I have my recipes and telephone numbers recorded on separate tapes. I keep a blank tape in the recorder just in case I need to record a new telephone number or a message.

When pouring coffee, water, or other juices I put my thumb on the edge and down a little bit into the cup or glass to tell when I have poured enough. I did this slowly at first but soon got the hang of it without any problem. I use this also when pouring milk into a bowl of cereal.

When ironing I place the garment over the ironing board and then smooth it with my hand before starting to iron. This keeps me from ironing wrinkles in the garment. This too, came easy and fast after a few times.

I have my husband pin his socks together after he takes them off, for the laundry.

Some people use round plastic cafe curtain rings. If he doesn't do this, I put his socks in a pile when I take them out of the dryer and he can match them and fold them himself. He has a choice.

I found that I had a hard time with my clothes and found some things to do that will help a lot. I keep a suit and the blouse to go with it hanging together. If there are more blouses that match the suit, they should be hanging with the suit also. I do slacks and sweaters this way too.

My shoes are kept on a rack in pairs. There is always something a little different about each pair that lets me know the difference in each pair. This also works for blouses. There is usually a difference in the sleeves, collar, placket, or buttons that will identify one blouse from the other.

The thing that I find the hardest to manage is to know if my hose have a runner. I usually ask my husband. The good ones I fold and the ones with a runner (that I wear under slacks) I tie into a knot.

Singer Sewing Company sells self-threading needles that I use. I sew on buttons and repair rips or tears and hem my slacks. This seems to be impossible, but after a few tries you can do it easily. They also have self-threading needles for sewing machines.

I have made a few garments, but it was frustrating and not fun anymore. So I watch the sales and buy my clothes. I find that the clerks in the dress shops are very helpful and willing to please. I have someone to go with me when I go to the discount stores where there are no clerks.

I have several white canes that I use. Each is a different length. I have a folding telescope cane which I use for church and restaurants. It folds nicely and fits into my purse. I have one two inches longer and another that comes to my shoulders.

The longer the cane, the faster I can walk. If the cane is too short I cannot find things in my way until I am upon them. It would be easy to fall over something if the cane is too short. These canes are fiber glass and light to the touch. I was told when I got mine that the cane would "talk" to me after awhile and really it does. I got mine from the National Federation of the Blind.

I joined the National Federation of the Blind and found it very helpful to be with other blind people. They can do so much for themselves and it makes me want to do just as well as they do. The NFB is blind people working with the blind and helping each other in many ways. There are other organizations for the blind but they are, for the most part, sighted people telling the blind what they need, don't need, and what they can and cannot do.

Blind people are not hiding in the closet like they were years ago. We are out there, doing the same things as sighted people. I have always been an independent person and I feel good about myself. My motto is: Don't give up, just keep on trying.

GROWING UP BLIND

by Jan Bailey

Jan Bailey is a rehabilitation counselor in Minnesota. It is not difficult to see why she has grown up to be such a well-adjusted, sensible person. Her parents deserve much of the credit for employing practical good sense and acting on their conviction that their little daughter was, when all was said and done, a normal child.

I am the fourth of nine children, and prior to my birth, my parents had very little knowledge about or exposure to blind people. I once asked my mother how she learned that I was blind. She told me that she took me for a check-up when I was four or five months old and mentioned to the doctor that I did not appear to look at things. He examined my eyes and told her that I was blind.

Afterward, my mother got on the streetcar to go home and suddenly began to panic. She wondered what she would do. For a split second she considered putting me down on the seat and leaving me there. Then, she remembered a blind man she had known. He had led a very normal life. He was married, had children, and held a job. She decided that if that was possible for him, then it would be possible for me.

My mother's experience illustrates my belief that it is desperately important for parents of blind children to have contact with capable blind adults. We can be role models for your children and can help you as that blind man helped my mother. The National Federation of the Blind is an excellent resource for parents because our membership is made up of thousands of blind people who are leading normal lives.

Like many parents, mine went from doctor to doctor trying to have my sight restored. Finally, when I was about a year old, my parents took me to a renowned specialist in Salt Lake City, Utah. The doctor examined me and then told my parents, "Quit going to doctors. There is nothing that can be done for your daughter's eyes. She will always be blind. Take her home and treat her just like the rest of your children." To the best of their ability, they did just that.

One of the first discoveries my parents made was that I was afraid of a number of things. I disliked anything fuzzy, I did not like loud noises, and I was terrified of the grass. My mother just kept exposing me to fuzzy objects, and one good thing came out of the fear before I was cured of it.

I had developed a habit of throwing my empty bottle out of the crib every night. Since they were made of glass, each night the bottle broke. My mother decided to remedy this situation by wrapping my bottle in a diaper and putting rubber bands around it, but I would have nothing to do with it. I was now afraid of my fuzzy bottle, and I never drank from one again. My mother, however, was persistent and kept exposing me to soft, fuzzy objects, and I soon outgrew that fear.

My mother thought that some of my fears developed because I did not see others around me handling objects. She also concluded that when I went to new places and heard noises I had never heard before, I was frightened because I couldn't associate the sound with anything I recognized. She kept exposing me to the things I was afraid of, explaining them and making me touch as many of them as possible.

She made a point of taking me everywhere and making me do things. She says I would have been perfectly content to sit in a corner and play, but she would not allow me to do so. She, my father, or one of my brothers or sisters would make me play with them.

Once my father had accepted my blindness, he decided to order some literature about blind children. He received a book in the mail that said: "Put your blind child in a cardboard box in a dark room. Your blind child is very fragile. Let your child explore the box and then the room."

My father threw that book away and told my mother that if that was what the experts had to say on the subject, he figured he could manage on his own. He said common sense told him that was the worst piece of advice he had ever received.

When I was two years old, I suddenly stopped talking. I had spoken a few words, but then I quit. After several days, my father said that he'd had enough. He went over to the high chair where I was sitting, picked me up, and sat me down hard. "Say Mama," he said. I said it. Then he picked me up again and sat me down hard and said, "Say Dada." I said it, and from then on I had no more difficulty talking.

At around the same time, my father told me that he was going to show me where things were in the house. He said that I could not be running into them and that I must learn my way around.

He took me through all of the rooms and showed me where everything was. Then he said, "Now, when I tell you 'Keep your eyes open,' you'll know that I mean to keep your feelers working and your smeller working and your ears working. It would sound funny if I said that, so you'll know what I mean when I tell you to keep your eyes open."

A short time later I came running into the dining room from the kitchen where I had been playing. I hit my forehead hard on the dining room table, fell down, and began to cry. My mother jumped up to comfort me, but my father told her to let him handle it.

He went over, picked me up, gave me a swat on my back end, and said "Now, don't you remember, I showed you where that table was. You can't be running into things. Next time, keep your eyes open." My mother told him she thought he was being too hard on me, but he said I had to learn.

I soon stopped crying and went back to playing. A few minutes later, I came running into the dining room again. My father said that you could hardly have put a hair between my forehead and that table before I swerved. I never ran into the table again.

As I mentioned earlier, I was terrified of the grass when I was a young child. Each time my mother went out to hang clothes, she took me with her and put me down on the lawn. I always crawled over onto the cement or gravel, preferring that to the grass.

Eventually my father told my mother that he was going to do something about the situation. He took me out to the back yard and proceeded to roll me around on the grass. I began to scream, and the neighbors came running. They told him that he was cruel, but he ignored them. He took me back into the house and told my mother not to say anything more about the grass.

I pouted for a few days before coming to my mother one day and asking for my hat and coat. That meant I wanted to go outside to play. She helped me to put on my things and watched me as I went out.

I went over to the grass and cautiously extended my toe and touched it. I waited for a second and then explored it with my foot. Soon I was rolling around on the lawn and after that had no fear of grass.

My father has often told me that when I was small, I had some rather strange ideas. One day I handed him a chicken bone from which I had eaten all the meat and asked him to put some more chicken on it. Another day I asked him to lift me up so I could touch the sky.

On such occasions he tried to explain the true nature of things so that I would not continue to have misconceptions about my surroundings. He did have quite a time, though, making me understand that I couldn't touch the sky, because he always made a point of letting me touch things in order for me to learn about them.

Once I wanted to touch an elephant at the zoo. My father persuaded the zoo keeper to let me go into the cage and touch it. He didn't want to give me special treatment, so he persuaded the poor keeper to let my brothers and sisters go in also.

When I was quite young, a woman from the welfare department who had learned I was blind came to visit my mother. She showed my mother a large wooden shoe and some pieces of cloth with buttons, buttonholes, and snaps on them. She tried to persuade my mother that she needed to purchase these things to teach me to tie my shoes, button my dress, and snap snaps.

My mother told her that first, she didn't have the money to buy those things, and second, she didn't see any need for them. She said that when I needed to learn these things, she would teach me using my own clothing.

When I was ready to go to kindergarten, I announced that I wanted to learn how to zip my jacket. I told her that I didn't want to have to ask the teacher to do it for me. I was to go to kindergarten at noon, and I pestered her all morning until I finally learned how to zip that jacket.

In the first grade I began to learn to read. I was very anxious to master this skill because I had heard some talking books, and I wanted to read just like the readers on the records.

One day, however, I came home from school in tears and told my parents that my teacher had said that I would not be allowed to check out library books while in first grade. My father could not understand this and so decided to phone the principal. Neither the principal nor the superintendent would overrule my teacher. So, my father called her directly. He tried calmly to persuade her that I should be allowed to check out library books. Finally in exasperation, he said, "Do you have any children?"

"No," said the teacher. "Well," he replied, "I have six of them, and I know that when children are anxious to learn, you shouldn't discourage them." But the teacher wouldn't be moved, so my father told me to go and talk to the librarian.

She asked me if I knew what a little white lie was. I told her I didn't. She said that it was a lie that wouldn't hurt anyone. She then told me to tuck a book under my coat and bring it back when I was finished reading it, and she would give me another one. I secretly read library books all during first grade.

Then there was the matter of my walking to school. I announced one day when I was six or seven years old that I thought I should be allowed to walk to school since my brothers and sisters could. Moreover, I wanted to walk by myself. I did not have a cane; back then children didn't use them.

My father said that he would show me the way to school, and I could go by myself. After a couple of weeks, I again announced one morning at breakfast that I wanted to walk to school by myself. My father replied that I had been doing so. "No, I haven't," I said. "You've been following me." He admitted that he had been, but he promised that that morning he would not. I could walk to school all by myself.

That night, I came home in tears and told my parents that the superintendent had come out to meet me at the driveway of the school when he saw that my father was not following me. That was not the end of it.

A few days later my father got a phone call. "Mr. Bailey," the superintendent said, "You are causing a problem in our school. You are allowing your daughter to walk to school by herself. She has told the other students about it, and now they want to do the same thing."

There were many other day students in town, and other parents were complaining. My father refused to comply with the request. He told the superintendent to tell those parents that they could raise their children the way they wanted to, and he would raise his the way he wanted.

At the age of seven or eight, I told my father I wanted to roller skate. He told me that he would take me out and put a pair of skates on me and take them off again, once. If I could get them back on, I could go skating. I don't suppose he thought I would be able to do it, but we went out and sat on the steps.

He showed me one time how to clamp the skates on, how to use a skate key, and how to buckle the straps. After he removed the skates, I put them back on myself. Then he told me I had some boundaries. I could go around the block. If I wanted to roller skate, I had to stay within my boundaries.

I skated for hours. That night, the neighbors complained about it. They told my father that it was dangerous and that I would hurt myself. They said it wasn't safe for me to go skating around the block by myself.

Again, my father ignored their advice. He told them that if I hurt myself too many times, I would give up roller skating. I did fall down repeatedly. In fact that first day, my legs were bleeding badly when I was through, but I persisted and soon rarely fell.

I also rode my tricycle around the block—another thing the neighbors didn't approve of. Soon, however, I wanted a bicycle. I worked hard to master the skill, but I soon tired of falling off and gave it up. I guess my father's theory was right. When I hurt myself enough, I made my own choices about what I would and could do.

At age ten or eleven, I became a Campfire Girl. Each year after that my sister and I went door to door selling candy. She went down one block, and I went down another.

One year we sold enough candy to earn a campship, which meant that since both of us planned to attend, our parents would have to pay half the cost for each of us. After we had successfully sold all of the candy, my Campfire leader told my parents that I would not be allowed to attend camp because I was blind. They pointed out that my sister could use the whole campship.

My father would have none of it. He told the Campfire officials that if I was good enough to sell their candy, then I was good enough to go to their camp. He suggested that they let me come to their camp, and if I caused any problems, he would come and pick me up. I went off to camp and had a great time.

When I was twelve or thirteen years old, I told my mother I wanted her to teach me how to iron. She said that I could not do so because I might burn myself. I recognized that she believed my blindness prevented my learning. This made me angry.

I went to my father and tried to get him to intervene, but this time he sided with my mother. One day when they had gone downtown, leaving my older sister in charge, I saw my opportunity. I told her that if she would show me how to iron, I would press all of her clothes. When my parents returned home, there I was, ironing. They never said another word about it.

We moved to Minnesota when I was twelve. There I attended the Minnesota Braille and Sight Saving School until I was a sophomore. That year I took half of my classes at the public high school. The next year I told my parents that I wanted to go to public school. Since we lived in Faribault, where the Braille School was located, the public school denied me entrance. They said that I would not be able to read the books in their library, and that I would use all of my energy trying to find my way around the school. I would be too tired to study.

I wrote to my state senator and representative, my United States senator, and to the governor of the state. But they all wrote back to say that they were sorry but my problem was out of their jurisdiction. Since my parents had very little extra money, they could not afford to hire a lawyer. I wish I had known then about the National Federation of the Blind. When I was going through that struggle, I felt very alone. I didn't know that other blind people had similar problems.

My parents heard that a Catholic school in Faribault (Bethelehem Academy) had enrolled deaf students since the public schools would not admit them either. My father and I went to Bethelehem Academy and persuaded the principal to admit me.

My parents had eight children at the time and did not have the two hundred dollars for my tuition. That summer my mother went to work in the corn canning plant to earn enough for my tuition and uniform, and in the fall I entered Bethelehem Academy, where I was on the honor roll.

When I graduated from college, my rehabilitation counselor encouraged me to go to graduate school to become one myself. I resisted doing this because I wanted to get a job in social work, for which I had been trained.

I think in the back of my mind I also wanted to know for a certainty that I could compete in something other than work with the blind.

Five years later I left Las Vegas where I had been working in a nursing home as a social worker and returned to Minnesota. I heard about a job opening in the Rochester district office of Minnesota State Services for the Blind, applied for it, and was hired. I decided to take that job because I knew that there are many blind people who have not had good opportunities and I wanted to help them have the chances I have had.

I realize that I was fortunate to have the parents I had, who taught me early in life that they had high expectations for me and that I could live a normal and productive life. That is my hope for all parents of blind children: that they will have high expectations for their children and that they will let them know they believe they can succeed.

President Marc Maurer and Executive Director Kenneth Jernigan present a National Federation of the Blind scholarship to Heidi.

ONE SMALL STEP AT A TIME

by Heidi Sherman

In 1988 Heidi Sherman received a college scholarship from the National Federation of the Blind. Today she is one of the leaders of the Federation's Student Division. She recently completed training at Blindness: Learning in New Dimensions (BLIND, INC.), the National Federation of the Blind's rehabilitation center in Minneapolis, Minnesota. Here is Heidi Sherman's account of learning how to tackle a job one small step at a time.

There are turning points in people's lives. Let me tell you about one in mine. It had to do with igniting a flame in a gas oven and, for me, it had to do with the rest of my life. It was an experience that reduced me to a gelatinous blob of helplessness.

I had just completed my rehabilitation training at BLIND, Inc., the National Federation of the Blind's Center in Minneapolis, Minnesota and returned home one cold Minnesota night to find that the exterminator had inadvertently extinguished the pilot light in my gas oven. How could he have known that such an innocent act could challenge all that I had fought for during the nine months that I had just spent at BLIND, Inc.?

When I got home that evening, I was very hungry, and I craved something hot—something that required a good searing in the oven. As I turned the temperature gauge, I noticed that the familiar whooshing sound of gas was curiously absent.

I stood there for what seemed an hour, and finally I realized that the pilot light must have somehow been extinguished. A parade of alternatives came to mind. Should I order out? Should I call the building manager and ask her to light the flame for me? Should I settle for a cold, unsatisfying sandwich? Or, should I just sit and starve?

The flame would have to be lit eventually since I couldn't order out every night. I cringed at the thought of calling the building manager and confirming her belief that blind people are incompetent. But I really wanted something hot in my stomach; so, if I couldn't have that, then I would have to settle for starvation unless I could manage to light the flame myself.

Peering into the shadowy cavern of the oven, I strained to see with my limited vision where the sound of the spewing gas was coming from. Throwing caution to the wind, I stuck my head into the oven thinking all the time of the witch in <u>Hansel and Gretel</u>.

In frustration I began to throw lighted matches at any little black opening I could distinguish. Ten minutes passed, and I withdrew my sore neck and blackened nose, sat back on my heels, and yelled in frustration. Turning off the gas, I sat paralyzed by my greatest fear—the fear that I could not do the thing facing me because of my blindness.

Beset by a black cloud of defeat, I suddenly had a realization, which gave me hope. I had been forgetting a major lesson of my training. At BLIND, Inc. I learned that a blind person can have a successful career, lobby for legislation, climb a mountain, or achieve anything else he or she wants.

The most important lesson, however, is that in order to reach these goals, you have to do the preliminary, usually small, things first. You can't raise a house without laying a foundation. You can't get a job without knowing how to sign your name.

And you certainly can't climb a mountain without first sweating in the foothills. In the National Federation of the Blind we talk about the importance of setting goals that are based on high expectations for ourselves, but these dreams will forever remain mere dreams if we can't muster the guts and determination to work toward them.

Switching on the gas, I inched forward and began feeling inside the oven. Very quickly I located the source of the gas and drew the lighted match to it, keeping my head well out of the oven. Like the sound of a roaring crowd, the flame ignited. This time my shout was one of joy. In great satisfaction I cooked the best meal that I had ever eaten.

AS MEAN AS MY MOM

by Dan Ryles

Dan Ryles is an active teenager who is one of a growing group of young people who have come to the National Federation of the Blind as children. They are growing up already knowing about blindness what it took many of us half a lifetime to learn. For a time Dan was nearly deaf as well as being totally blind, but much of his hearing has been restored through surgery. Dan's mother, Ruby, is a leader in the Federation's Parents Division. This is what Dan had to say when he spoke to that group.

My family moved to the Seattle area the summer before my eighth grade year. I was, and still am, the only blind kid in my school district, and the teachers and students had little or no experience with blind people before I enrolled. The kids' preconceptions about blindness, along with the normal junior high mentality, made the first semester exceptionally difficult.

Not many people spoke to me or had much to do with me. Of course, there were those few who constantly hung around me wanting to know exactly how I did everything.

I could live with that, but what hurt me were the times spent getting dressed and undressed for gym class in the locker room. Surely most of you remember what eighth grade locker room talk is like. Much of it is obscene and very cruel. My blindness seemed to make me the perfect target for insults and ridicule.

I couldn't cry in front of the kids, but I did cry on occasion at home. Even my new girl friend had lots of negative attitudes, which were painful to me.

The science teacher took it upon himself to decide for me what assignments I could and could not do, never considering the possible adaptations I might make. I knew his attitudes were not good when on the first day of class he assumed I would need to tape his lectures instead of Brailling notes with my slate and stylus.

Those were hard times, but my mom helped me through them with the philosophy of the National Federation of the Blind. She told me that the things the kids said weren't really true. Junior high kids will find something wrong with everyone, and they will

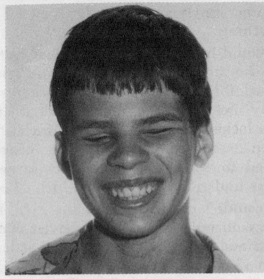

Dan doesn't let blindness dampen his spirits.

greatly exaggerate it. My blindness was the most obvious characteristic they could see.

I have come a long way since then. The kids have gradually come to accept me. This last year (my ninth grade year) I took algebra, Spanish, chemistry, American history, English, and symphonic band. I would never have gotten to where I am today if my mom had not had the necessary reading and writing skills to teach me when everyone else was learning them in print.

I also learned basic cane skills in first and second grade. That may seem early when compared to some kids' experience, but not as early as I should have been taught it. If I had had a cane in preschool, things would have been a lot easier. The earlier you teach a kid cane skills, the sooner he can travel independently.

Now I can travel as well as anyone and have a daily paper route, which brings in $120 a month. I do the route entirely on my own, including collections, for which I Braille the receipts.

I was lucky. I had a mom who didn't over-protect me. I did, and still do, occasionally scrape a knee or bruise an elbow. I once even had stitches in my head, but that's just a natural part of growing up. It has nothing to do with my blindness. This may sound a little crude, but if you'll be as mean as my mom, your blind kid will be okay.

A BLIND TEACHER ON THE JOB

by Judy Krecek

Sometimes we forget how much encouragement we can give one another just by sharing our reflections on our own jobs. It can also happen that talking with others about our work provides us with new insights and perspectives on our lives. Recently, Judy Krecek, a member of the Kankakee-Heartland Chapter of the National Federation of the Blind of Illinois, spoke to her chapter about her job as a teacher. Each meeting of the National Federation of the Blind (whether at the local, the state, or the national level) is a time for sharing, reinforcement, and encouragement.

When people ask me why I am a teacher, sometimes I answer, "June, July, and August." But, of course, that's not really true, I love teaching. I can touch children's lives and make a difference. Even if I help only one child in twenty years, I feel my work has been successful.

When I was young, I played school. I think maybe I went into teaching because of my family. Neither of my parents had a happy childhood. My father grew up in an orphanage. For that reason he made sure that our family was very close. My mother was unloved and was encouraged not to further her own education, so education and affection were very important to her.

I spent my early years in a class for blind children, but they did not teach Braille, which was a big mistake. In fact, I did not learn Braille until I was in college. I did not enjoy my experience in school, for I was pulled out of regular class and sent to the special education class. I was encouraged not to play with the regular kids, and I was basically segregated from the mainstream.

In the sixth grade this program deteriorated because the teacher said that I should be able to read large print books as fast as the regular kids. Never mind that I had several eye problems. I ran home to my mother and told her that the teacher said my IQ was okay, but I failed every test I had taken because I could not read very fast and sometimes not at all. The truth was that no one knew Braille, so I was not taught, and as a result I was set up to fail. I simply could not see.

My mother tutored me in the subjects I was lacking, and everything was better. In those days, when a blind student went to private school, there were no materials, so my mother bought a tape recorder she could not afford and read all my books for me.

She continued doing all of my reading through college and even typed my Latin in large print. If I had not had a mom like that, I would not have made it through the system. Mom had three other kids, so she was very busy. She was invaluable to me.

In high school I would sleep only three or four hours per night because it took me so long to complete my assignments; I simply could not see. This is why Braille is so important. I could not keep up using print. When I was sixteen, my mother asked if I wanted to quit because it was such a strain. Of course I did not.

When I was ten I did get a Talking Book Machine, but we had to fight for it. They said they did not have children's books and that if I had the machine I might not push myself to read. Again, I did not read because I could not see, but no one realized this.

When it came time to decide about college, I had my mother's support, but my father thought it unnecessary. Of course, now he brags about how I have two degrees. At that time I think my father was afraid of what would happen in a new situation.

When it was time for student teaching, I was told I could not do it. The woman in charge said that she had wanted to be a doctor but that we do not always get what we want. She said she would not want her child in my class for safety reasons. I did not know how to answer. They made me teach on campus, but I did do it. They gave me a rough time, but I still got the license.

I have had several parents who wanted to pull their children out of my class because it was too hard, but not because of blindness. I have always talked these parents out of moving their children.

It is good for everyone to have challenging classes. What I am trying to tell you is that when you meet the people in your life who tell you that you cannot do something, you have to prove them wrong. All the way through school people would say that they admired my enthusiasm, but.... When people say "but," it is time for combat.

I had many interviews when I was looking for my first job. On my license one line stated that I was blind. When the interviewers read that, there were all kinds of excuses about why they did not need me.

I had a lot of rejections before I got my first job. The only reason I got the job I did was that Latin was my minor and the district was desperate for a Latin teacher. The superintendent offered me the job on the spot. It was August, and he needed a teacher that day.

He asked if I had any questions, and I said that I did not but that he had not asked about my blindness. He simply asked if I thought I could teach, and of course I said I could. He said that was all that he wanted to know. I was thrilled because I was going to earn real money, $5,300 a year.

I do love my job. The first day of class I always tell my students in what ways I proceed differently. I work from recorded tests. I have the students listen to prerecorded stories, which they love. When a student needs help with pronunciation, I instruct that student to spell the word rather than point.

Even though the students know that I am blind, they ask what kind of car I drive because everyone in their world drives. I have to remind them that blind people do not drive.

Of course, my students pull pranks, but they are all out of love. One day they turned my desk around so that, when I sat down, I banged my knees. They just wanted to know how I would react. We talked about people's feelings and how we must respect one another. I give them assigned seats and tell them why, and I hire a reader to do some of my grading. Also I teach computers and use one myself. I got roped into teaching the class because I had the skill.

I have two classes of three hours each— language arts, social studies, etc. Using the computers has really helped my students' writing skills. Every year I have them participate in the young author's contest, which is quite a challenge. I also use my talking clock calculator, which has other features as well.

A lot of people think that I am smart, but I, like many, have to work hard at my job. I insist on the best from my students. I know that the results are worth the struggle. One problem I see these days is that they want to give up too easily. I do my best to encourage them to keep on trying.

Blindness does make for more challenges, but we all know that. All people face challenges; being blind simply makes them obvious. I have worked now for twenty-four years, and I have been happy to have a job that is very, very rewarding.

ACCENTUATE THE POSITIVE

by Shirley Baillif

How do you face the fact that your child is blind? How do you answer his questions? What advice do you give him? Where do you find hope? How much does your son learn from you—and how much do you learn from him? Here is how it happened with Shirley Baillif, who lives in California and who came to the state convention of the National Federation of the Blind to tell her story.

Years ago there was a popular song that said in part:

You've got to accentuate the positive,
Eliminate the negative,
Latch on to the affirmative,
And don't mess with Mr. In-between.

If I were asked to give one piece of advice on raising a blind child, that little ditty would express my philosophy.

When our son became totally blind at age thirteen, one month before entering high school, we felt terrified—lost in a situation we knew little or nothing about. When Michael, who was an active teenager, more interested in sports than academics, turned to me and said, "Mom, what will I do now?" The Good Lord gave me the sense not to see a dismal picture of a young boy growing old, helplessly striving to eke out a living. Instead I answered him honestly by saying in effect, "Michael, I have never known a blind person well enough to know how the blind accomplish the tasks they do, but I have encountered a few blind people indirectly, and I know they have not only graduated from high school, but gone on to graduate from college, become professionals in various fields, or build their own businesses. Honey, if they can do it, so can you—you just have to learn how." And that is exactly what we set out to do.

As soon as Michael was released from the hospital, I called our local high school, explained the situation, and received a response of absolute dismay. This was a new situation to them. The few blind students they had had in the past came to the high school from the elementary program, where they had learned basic skills and they had no idea how they would teach a blind student. Fortunately, we found two positive-

Shirley Baillif's son Michael today: President of the National Federation of the Blind Student Division and a student at Yale University School of Law.

thinking special teachers who were able to help with Braille and mobility.

All through his high school years, I was told that I should protest if Michael wasn't getting the help he should have. But how could I protest something I knew little or nothing about? I wish we had known about the National Federation of the Blind then.

Our family was introduced to the NFB when Michael was searching for college scholarships. Michael is not a joiner. He made one exception, though. After receiving a scholarship from the NFB he felt obligated to give back $5.00 of it and become a member of the Student Division. It turned out to be the best investment he ever made or ever will.

There is no way I can even begin to express how much the NFB has meant to our family or how much Michael has been influenced by the positive role models of the NFB leaders, both on the state and national levels. And I cannot tell you how much his peers within the Federation have become, not only special friends of Michael's, but like a close-knit family to his father and me. We watch their lives unfold as they strive for and accomplish their individual goals, overcoming the stumbling blocks that have been thrown in their paths.

I have learned so much since those days spent with Michael at UCLA's Jules Stein Eye Institute, and now I want to share this knowledge with other parents as they come face to face with the destinies of their blind offspring. This is why I am so excited about starting a support group for Parents of Blind Children in our area. I have a young mother of a newly blinded child, whom I met through a mutual friend, to thank for showing me this need; and I have the NFB to thank for giving me the encouragement and positive attitude to meet it.

BACK TO NOTRE DAME

by Marc Maurer

From the Editor: Marc Maurer is totally blind. He is a successful lawyer. He has a wife and two small children who are not blind—a boy (David Patrick) and a girl (Diana Marie). He is paying on a mortgage and looking to the future with hope—but it was not always that way. He was struggling to find himself and wondering if he could have a meaningful life.

When I left the Presidency of the National Federation of the Blind in 1986, Marc was elected as my successor. At the convention the following year he told the members something about his reasons for becoming a lawyer.

As I was growing up, I (like all others, blind and sighted alike) was conditioned by my culture and society. I hoped that there would be something interesting or important for me to do, but I was afraid that blindness might keep me from it. When I came to the Federation, I found blind people working and making substantive contributions.

I was told that blindness need not be a terrible limitation. I hoped that the Federation was right, but I had doubts. Nevertheless, I said that I believed, and I tried to act as though I did. It was only later that I realized (with something of a shock) that the belief had come to be a reality in my life—and a good while before I recognized it.

Dr. Jernigan taught me about blindness and the organized blind movement—and there were others. I talked with blind people who were lawyers, teachers, factory workers, and farmers. At Federation meetings blind leaders spoke of the power of collective action.

Soon I began to repeat what those around me were saying: that blindness could be reduced to the level of a physical nuisance, that with proper training and opportunity the average blind person could do the average job in the average place of business—in short that it was respectable to be blind.

Then, I went to college at Notre Dame—and it was a sudden plunge into ice water. On a campus with six thousand other students, I found myself completely isolated and alone. I could not find a single other person who understood what I thought I understood or believed what I said I believed, the simple truth that blind people had capacity and could compete.

The Maurers—She reads to her children from a Braille storybook, and he charcoals the burgers—an ordinary American family.

I met no one else who thought it was respectable to be blind. The coach in the athletic department told me that I should not take any gym classes because I might get hurt. When signing up for an accounting course, I was praised by the professor for my great courage. Then (without even changing gears) the professor promised me a good grade.

I got the idea that I did not have to earn it, that just being there and being courageous would be enough. I worked hard to deserve that grade, and I worked hard for the other grades I got, too. It was an unforgettable experience; and although I have physically returned to that campus only once since graduation, I have (in one way of speaking) been back to Notre Dame many times through the years.

That first semester I learned with real force (I might say with dramatic force) that blindness could not stop me, but I also learned that prejudice and misunderstanding might. Something had to be done. The situation was intolerable.

All of those professors and students had to be told. I needed help. I needed the National Federation of the Blind. As the years at the university passed, I became increasingly active in our movement. My priorities crystallized and became clear.

After college I did graduate work, and in 1977 I finished law school. In 1978, with the help of Federation members, I got a job in the office of the General Counsel at the Civil Aeronautics Board. With my philosophy and idealism in hand, I went to that job willing and anxious to work.

I wanted to give of my time, my effort, and my energy. I wanted to advance myself and the cause of the blind. The Civil Aeronautics Board made United States civil aviation policy. Here, I thought, is an opportunity for me to do something really useful.

However, I soon discovered that a pattern existed—a pattern which reminded me of the professor who told me that I was courageous, and promised me a good grade. I felt right at home. It was just like being back at Notre Dame.

My assignments were almost always routine. If there was a trip to London for an international negotiation, somebody else was asked to go. If a hearing officer needed to take testimony in a small town to determine the feasibility of air service, I was never sent. These assignments (calculated to vary the routine) were highly prized and much sought after. Others went while I stayed home—and was courageous.

Sometimes there was not enough routine work to fill my day. So I was left to occupy my time as I chose. My superiors would have been content if I had spent my time listening to the radio or reading. They would have been content—but I would not have been content.

I did not want the rest of my life to be a sham and a deception, a guaranteed succession of endless raises and lack of meaningful work. Discrimination is not necessarily confined to the job interview or the entry level. It can also happen after employment is permanent and safe.

My job with the federal government was absolutely secure. It would have lasted until retirement through a long and rustful life. There was something else: we all tend to be conditioned by our environment. I knew that if I stayed long enough and my salary became high enough, I might become accustomed to the lack of useful activity and gradually lose my initiative, my sense of values, my perspective, my willingness to leave, and my soul.

Not only had the Federation taught me about blindness but also about self-examination, objectivity, and perspective. In 1981 I left the Civil Aeronautics Board to start my own law practice.

I knew that I might starve, but I also knew that if I starved, it would be a starvation of the body and not of the soul. I knew that I would be free, and not a token or a cipher.

Slavery does not have to be a matter of chains and whips. It can also be a captivity of the mind and a shackling of the spirit. Every person in this room can give testimony to that. We in the Federation have cut our teeth on it, and we never stop learning it.

On a daily basis we continue to teach it to ourselves and each other, and we give it in strong doses to new recruits. This is why some, who do not understand our philosophy, call us militant.

In the practice of law my dream that I might do something worthwhile and useful came true.

I WAS FORTY-THREE...

by Edgar Sammons

As Executive Director of the National Federation of the Blind I receive many letters. Some are encouraging; others heartrending. But I think I have never received a more expressive and revealing letter than the one I am about to share with you. It was written by Edgar Sammons, who lives in Mountain City, Tennessee, and speaks with the language and clarity of Elizabethan prose. I have never met Edgar Sammons, but I have thought long about his letter and have come to feel a deep affection and high respect for him. He is not a complainer, not a whiner—but he has known custody, terrible loneliness, blighted hope and real deprivation. Yet, he has made a life for himself. His letter is as significant for what it does not say as for what it says.

I thought I would give you a little history of my life. I was born October 30, 1913. They said I lost my sight at three weeks old. I grew just like the rest of them. I think a blind person should be brought up just like a sighted person but most of them are not. Most of them would learn a lot more if they would let them. We just had an old boxed house and a little land. Not enough to make a living on. My father always rented corn ground for half of it. My mother put up a lot of stuff, and we always had plenty to eat.

My father worked on the first highway that come through here. They blacktopped it in 1924. *[I interrupt the letter to point out that he is now eleven years old, and this is the first thing that has happened to him that he feels worth noting.]*:

My father rented a little farm, and we moved to it. It was not very far from here. We lived there a year and moved back.

My mother always wanted to send me to school, but my father never would give up for it. My grandmother and my mother and little baby sister all died in 1924. There were five of us children left. Some people wanted to put us in a home.

We had a hard time, but we made out. If the family could have had their way I don't guess I would have been allowed to get off the place without some one of them with me. They couldn't watch me all of the time.

My grandmother Sammons was still living and they would send me down there when they would go to work in the corn. That suited me just fine. My grandmother would be doing her housework, and I would go down the road about half a mile to my aunt's and stay a while. Sometimes some of them would find it out and tell on me, but I didn't care what they done about it. I would run off every chance I got. There was just mud roads, but I got along.

They would take me places with them at night. They went a lot of places at that that I would have like to have went, but they left me at my grandmothers. I think the blind should be allowed to get out and learn to get around just like the sighted when they are growing up. A lot of us don't have that chance.

My brother and father went to work in a cotton mill at Johnson City, and we moved down there in 1927. *[He was born in 1913, so he is now fourteen years old.]* The mill closed down in 1928, and we moved back. *[Now, he's fifteen.]* In 1933 *[He's now twenty.]* all of the children got off over at Ashville, North Carolina, and got jobs. *[You notice that he didn't get a job.]*

My father married again in 1933. I stayed at home most of the time. After that my job in the summertime was pasturing the cows in the road. I had bells on them so I could tell where they was at. I set on the banks with the cows, wondering how I could get a little money to get some tobacco. I was a young man then.

The welfare started in 1937. *[He's now twenty-four.]* I got a little. A lot of blind didn't get any. There wasn't very much work for the blind then. I would go to Ashville and stay a while and come back here and stay a while.

In 1944 *[He's now thirty-one.]* I went to Ashville and got me a job sorting mica. *[Remember: This is his first job. It was the Second World War, and manpower was scarce. But back to his letter]*: They said we would do the job better than the sighted people. I just got to work nine weeks, and our part of the job closed down. I stayed a while longer over there to see if it would start back up, but it never did.

That was a good job, but in one way I didn't like it. I stayed with my sister and her husband. They were as good to me as they could be, but they wanted me with them all the time. They would come after me at night and take me to work in the morning. I didn't want that. I wanted out on my own like other people. I wanted to get out and get me a girl just like other people.

Well, I come back home and stayed around here most of the time. My stepmother died in 1951. *[Now, he's thirty-eight.]* Grady Weaver started teaching me to read and write Braille in 1951. I can't spell very good, but that helped some. I stayed at home with my father until 1957. *[His life is passing. He's now forty-four.]* My father got so bad sick that they put him in a rest home, and I went to Morristown and got me a job in the sheltered workshop.

Mattie Ruth was working there at that time. She told someone, 'the Sammons has come; the bass will be here next.' Sure enough in a few days a man did come by the name Bass.

Just a little while after I went to work, Mattie Ruth got sick and went home. She like to have died. She didn't come back any more for about three years. She worked for a while, and her father got sick and she went home to take care of him. He died in 1962. *[Now, he's forty-nine.]*

After that, I went up and got Mattie Ruth. Her mother said she ought to have run me off the first time I ever come up there. She said I took the last girl she had.

I was forty-three years old before I got out on my own, but it has been the best part of my life. If I had stayed with my people, I don't guess I would have been living by now. I didn't have anything to live for.

That is the letter. In a very real sense Edgar Sammons speaks for all blind people. The imprisonment and lack of opportunity were just as cruel as if they had been deliberately imposed. They were just as degrading, just as blighting, and just as painful.

We must see that it never happens again. That is why we have to strengthen the National Federation of the Blind and why we have to speak out. Our climb up the stairs to freedom has been slow and difficult, but we are nearing the top. We carry with us a trust for Edgar Sammons, and for all of the others who went before us. We also carry a trust for those who will follow—for the blind of the decades ahead.

National Federation of the Blind
YOU CAN HELP US...

- Publicize our nationwide annual contest (similar to a summer reading program for sighted children through a local public library) which encourages blind children to compete against one another in the reading of pages of Braille books.

- Publicize our scholarship program for deserving blind students.

- Make books about the capabilities of blind persons available to local public libraries of schools and universities, and distribute films and other literature about positive attitudes about blindness for school and other gatherings.

- Recruit volunteers interested in reading or driving for blind persons, or assisting with shopping needs.

- Conduct or attend Job Opportunities for the Blind (JOB) seminars for prospective blind employees and job applicants to teach the skills of resume writing, job hunting, interviewing, and choosing the appropriate field of work.

- Plan seminars for prospective employers of blind persons to broaden employers' awareness of the capabilities of blind persons and to help eliminate artificial barriers and unfounded prejudice about employing the blind.

WE CARE ABOUT YOU TOO!

If a family member, friend, or someone you know needs assistance with problems of blindness, please write:

Marc Maurer, President
1800 Johnson Street, Suite 300,
Baltimore, MD 21230-4998
You contribution is tax-deductible.